AGAIN I
HEAR THESE
WATERS

POEMS BY

HAFIZ AHMED
SHALIM M. HUSSAIN
KAZI NEEL
SHAJAHAN ALI AHMED
ASHRAFUL ISLAM
ABDUR RAHIM
SIRAJ KHAN
ABDUL KALAM AZAD
JOHIRUL ISLAM

AGAIN I HEAR

THESE WATERS

CURATED BY SHALIM M. HUSSAIN

RAFIQUL ISLAM
REJAUL ISLAM BULBUL
ABDUL MOZID SHEIKH
MOHIN KHAN
RINGKUL AHMED
AMAN ALI
REHNA SULTANA
GAZI RAHMAN
MIRZA LUTFAR RAHMAN
HEENA AL HAYA
AMEENA AHMED
BEGUM ASMA KHATUN

TILTED AXIS PRESS

CONTENTS

This book is for Assam, our home.

INTRODUCTION

This anthology of translated poems and songs comes from the 'Miyah' community of the Northeast Indian state of Assam. Except for Hafiz Ahmed's 'Write Down "I am Miyah"', all of the poems were originally written in Assamese or the local dialects spoken by the community. This story of this community is tied to the history of modern India. Present-day Assam shares an international border with Bangladesh. Historically, Assam has seen multiple waves of migration. However, during the rule of the British Raj in the nineteenth century, the government facilitated the migration of a large agricultural labour community, predominantly Muslim, into Assam from areas which now fall in Bangladesh. This class of labourers were the ancestors of the 'Miyahs'.

They settled mostly in the low-lying riverine areas, demarcated by the administration as 'wastelands', and grew rice and jute. Both these crops feature heavily in this anthology. The areas they settled in, *chars* and *chaporis,* unstable islands and riverbanks of the Brahmaputra River, were always at the mercy of floods and erosion – the twin natural disasters that visit Assam every year. However, the terrain was not unknown to them because the areas they migrated from were the same. Over time their population grew but a major chunk of it continued living in the char-chaporis, facing the same ravages of nature their ancestors had faced. This is why the themes of the folk river-songs in this anthology carry over so easily to the poems. One of the terms the community still uses to identify itself is 'char-chapori people', a people defined by their immediate geography. In this anthology the islands and riverbanks keep reappearing, both as background and metaphor. And like poetry and songs from most working-class communities, the poems in this anthology glamourise labour, particularly tough physical labour which can bend the world and nature to its will.

The word 'Miyah' itself is derogatory street slang with implications of barbarism and otherness. Originally a respectful term of address, no one knows when it began to be used in a negative sense for the 'char-chapori people' in Assam. In April 2016, the poet Hafiz Ahmed wrote the poem 'Write Down "I am Miyah"' modelled on Mahmoud Darwish's 'Identity Card'. The poem highlighted the problem with the term 'Miyah' while at the same time reclaiming it. This was not the first time a 'Miyah' poet declared themselves Miyah but it made other poets from the community respond to this poem through their own poems. Some of the responses are included in this anthology. A journalist called this collection of responses 'Miyah poetry' and that's where the term had its genesis. A corpus of rich 'char-chapori poetry' existed in Assam three decades before 'Miyah poetry' started and continues to grow to this day but most of these poets didn't identify as 'Miyah poets'.

Miyah poetry started as political poetry, responding to the then current issues of the National Register of Citizens or NRC which was being updated only for the residents of Assam and the Foreigners' Tribunals. The former was an exercise to identify illegal immigrants resident in Assam. The latter was a quasi-judicial body that has the power to identify 'foreigners' or illegal immigrants. 'Declared foreigners' could be sent to detention centres. Initially many of the poets challenged the heavy-handedness of these processes. The NRC was updated and a final draft was published in 2019 but it was not enacted.

'Miyah poetry' today can still be political though the immediate context in which it began is gone. However, there is much more to the poems by these poets. Hafiz Ahmed's 'Babajaan' is a history of the community through multiple generations. Kazi Neel's poems recreate the horror of the 1990s in Assam with literally chilling images. There's a feeling of loss, loneliness and fear in his poems which is shared by Ashraful Islam, Shajahan Ali Ahmed and Abdul Kalam Azad. Abdur Rahim, Siraj Khan, Johirul Islam and Rafiqul Islam all write with passion but their hard-hitting poems are filled with deep yearning. Someone has described Miyah poetry as 'yearning to belong' and I think it's quite true. Mohin Khan and Rehna Sultana's poems are deep and moving, so much so that I had a difficult task translating them because of how personal and sensitive they were. The poems in this collection are ordered in the manner in which I translated them. The newest poems, written by Ameena Ahmed and Begum Asma Khatun are an indication of the new direction Miyah poetry has taken. Miyah poetry is moving from the particular into the wholeness of experience.

Shalim M. Hussain, curator and translator

WRITE DOWN 'I AM A MIYAH'

Hafiz Ahmed

Write

Write Down
I am a Miyah
My serial number in the NRC is 200543.
I have two children.
Another is coming next summer.

Will you hate him as you hate me?

Write
I am a Miyah

I turn waste, marshy lands
to green paddy fields
            to feed you.

I carry bricks
to build your buildings.

Drive your car
for your comfort.

Clean your drain
to keep you healthy.

I have always been in your service
and yet you are dissatisfied!

Write down
I am a Miyah,

A citizen of a democratic, secular, Republic
without any rights.
My mother is a D voter,
though her parents are Indian.
If you wish, kill me, drive me from my village,
snatch my green fields
and hire bulldozers to roll over me.
Your bullets can shatter my breast for no crime.

Write
I am a Miyah
of the Brahmaputra
Your torture has burnt my body black
and reddened my eyes with fire.

Beware!

I have nothing but anger in stock.
Keep Away!
or turn to Ashes.

BABAJAAN

Hafiz Ahmed

1
Just like in the movies
Every word you say
Becomes an incident,
A wave in my mind
This dark night.

2
The incident of 1950
When you built a banana raft
And kept it ready on the Bhelengi
So that if needed we could
Take to the Brahmaputra and save our lives

3
Babajaan and his people
Didn't have to leave
Dhaniram Talukdar of Barpeta said,
'Why will you leave?
Is this land not yours?
Didn't you turn this mother's heart fertile
With the sweat of your brow?'

4

Babajaan didn't leave
But Nanajaan did
He left this land
Not for the land downstream
But for the eternal emptiness beyond.
One evening he was on his patch of green land
In Bogulimari
Mashing rice and milk and ripe plantain
And raising a morsel to his mouth
When an enemy newly arrived from downstream
Swung once his sword
And Nana's head was on the ground.

On that day a pact was made.
Our king and they who had come for refuge from downstream
Made an agreement.

5

Just as a hen collects her chicken
Under her wings
Our Nanajaan bound my uncles and aunts
In his shawl and sent them downstream
They returned eventually but by then
The counting of humans was over
And our uncles and aunts were left out.

6

They were lovers of green fields –
My uncles and aunts
And an intoxication was upon them.

They cleared forests and bared the earth's chest
And as the green turned golden
They sang Magun and Bihu
And started the harvest.

7

The storm of time returned
Some PIP or something
What was it called?
Because their names were missing
From the list of humans
They were bound up again
And sent downstream.

8

Babajaan, Majaan
And our aunts
Were safe
But only for a while

The dark clouds of time
Gathered again –
And one day we heard
That our aunt, married in Nellie,
Was still wrapped in a green sari
Still holding her five month daughter on her breast,
When the guns came
And granted her eternal peace.

9

And then Babajaan left

10
Maybe Babajaan was safer
In the lap of death

Or else he might have been
Felled by militants
In Bashbari, Kokrajhar, Khagrabari

Or

His long beard
And green lungi
And broken Assamese
Might have prompted some
Patriot to make him sit on his knees
In the sun
Or like Jabbar Ali he might
Have been called a foreigner
In his own country and made to rot
And die in jail.

11
We are not as scared
As you were, Babajaan
You said, 'Learning is light
Burn the lights of knowledge
And the demons will scatter.'
I followed your advice
And am not scared of demons anymore.
Kalam, Dwijen, Tridip and I and many others
Will fight together

And prove that this land
Is not of the masked patriots alone.
This land is not of attackers alone.
This land is the land of your blood and sweat.

NANA I HAVE WRITTEN

Shalim M. Hussain

Nana I have written attested countersigned and been verified
by a public notary that I am a Miyah
now see me rise from flood waters, float over landslides
march through sand and marsh and snakes
break the earth's will draw trenches with spades
crawl through fields of rice and diarrhoea and sugar cane
and a 10% literacy rate
See me shrug my shoulders curl my hair
read two lines of poetry one formula of math
read confusion when the bullies call me Bangladeshi
and tell my revolutionary heart
But I am a Miyah
See me hold by my side the Constitution
point a finger to Delhi walk to my Parliament my Supreme
Court my Connaught Place
and tell the MPs the esteemed judges and the lady selling
trinkets and her charm on Janpath
Well I am Miyah.
Visit me in Kolkata in Nagpur in the Seemapuri slums
see me suited in Silicon Valley suited at McDonald's
enslaved in Beerwa bride-trafficked in Mewat

see the stains on my childhood these gold medals on my PhD
certificate
then call me Salma call me Aman call me Abdul call me
Bahaton Nessa
or call me Gulam.
See me catch a plane get a Visa catch a bullet train
catch a bullet
catch your drift
catch a rocket
wear a lungi to space
and there where no one can hear you scream,
Thunder
I am Miyah
I am Proud

MY LOVE'S LETTERS

Shalim M. Hussain

May the rain not soak my love's letters
May my love be a shield
May my love be silk
May my love's new wings shield my love's letters,

May the sun be softer
May the clouds be lighter
May it rain less this year
May the eaves drip less
And the waters spare my love's letters.

Let the river swell, let jute soak
Let bridges come up and prove inadequate
Let my love's father and my love's brothers
Play ludo and snakes in the shade
Let man and woman and woman and child not huddle
Under a rain that could wet my love's letters

Let the river swell, let jute soak
Let sugarcane grow thick
Under the leaves, with my head on her heart

May I still feel the edges
Of my love's letters.

May the letters still say that she was born
That she grew, that she married
That she lives, that she is.
May they not come undone on her lips
Crinkle under her fingernails
Get lost in her hair.
May not her breath set them on fire.

May not the mist find them
May not a landslide take them
May not the river carry away
My love's letters.

REPUBLIC'S BROKEN WALL

Kazi Neel

Poor Republic
Breaks stones on the Panchmile hill
And picks scraps in Barowari bazaar.

Poor Republic's
House is on the river's edge
Water drips down Republic's roof.

Republic works in Other lands
Sleeps on footpaths
Republic's throat cracks with a Republic thirst.

Republic's dark house and broken walls –
A fox sneaks in through the cracks.
Republic lies awake with a fever
A grim-quack sits by Republic's bed.

Poor Republic labours
And asks for two handfuls of rice –
They find *jaat paat* under Republic's lungi.

Lonely Republic's
Hunger burns in Republic's stove.
Republic is lame and maimed
Someone crushes Republic in a mortar's nook.

Poor Republic
    breaks stones on the Panchmile hill
Poor Republic
    picks scraps in every bazaar.

JOURNEY

Kazi Neel

I walk through half village, half town –
overhead, the cheap sky of a rain shop
and on the little houses by the roadside
one hundred years of darkness frozen to ice;
pond and lake drowned in rain.
Rain washes me inside out;
in my mind cotton drops float like frozen cries.

i walk through darkness, slip and fall –
death keeps sleeping in that hole.
i rise with a pain as fatal as death
and limp through a low-cost city.

i walk and think of a bird
on a dried-up branch in a rainless city.
i forget darkness, i forget my broken feet
i forget this cheap sky, my boyhood pains
my hungry youth.
i forget and forget and go blind
and the fear of falling in a hole is gone.

i have promised the bird the soul of a tree.
even if it has no leaf and no branch,
i will guard it like the shadow of death
and when all the dark nights of her town is done
i will come by the morning train,
trampling a mountain of mist.
my journey will not be like other sub-plots.

i know that this darkness, this typhoon, this deathly cold is
nothing
i will have to cross the great ocean of troubles,
rumble through the centuries like a demon.

i have promised to return
with the wet taste of rain in my heart
and all the leaves and branches of a garden.
with the croaking of frogs in heat
i will enter her town's port like an ancient sailor.

i walk through half village half town
i limp with a pain like death;
overhead the cheap sky of a rain shop.
in my mind frozen cries float like cotton drops.

oh woman, when kadam flowers ripen
a lone koel will call.
a wind from a faraway sea will blow your clothes
and i will come by the morning train.

COMRADE

Kazi Neel

Hussain Miyah rode a bicycle
The handlebars had two red flags,
Hammers and sickles. In a glimmer
Hussain Miyah cycled through fifty years,
Through villages and zig-zag paths.

Hussain Miyah took the aisle through mustard fields
When he came to our village
Children ran behind his cycle screaming
'Comrate. Comrate!'

Hussain Miyah knew no revolution
He had no Marx. What Lenin blabbered about,
From which land came Ho Chi Minh –
Hussain Miyah had no clue.

Hussain Miyah didn't know if you ate
Dialectic materialism or rubbed it on your scalp.
Hussain Miyah knew nothing except
That the red party was for the poor.

Hussain Miyah knew whose blood
The topi-wearing leaders sucked,
Hussain Miyah knew that the land was of workers –
The Land Was of Blood and Sweat
Every year the votes came and Hussain Miyah's
Clothes turned red.
Someone drew a hammer
and a sickle
on his chest
from river bank to river bank
came the tinkling of his bell.

'There goes Hussain Miyah, there's his raised fist!
Lal Salaam Lal Salaam!'

For ten years I have not seen Hussain Miyah –
Since the cold morning he came coughing.
He ate two handfuls of rice with a koi fish
And raised an ameen.

Sometimes I wake up in the middle of the night –
A cycle comes pedalling through my dreams,
Red flags on the handlebars,
And voices crying, 'Lal Salaam, Lal Salaam!'

SOMEONE WALKS BY

Kazi Neel

Something rustles in the backyard
Someone walks by the peak of night.
It's a cold cold January in the rice fields
Someone climbs a mountain of mist.
My hands shake, my feet tremble
Someone taps on the bamboo wall
A voice slips on the air – Rahim *ka*!
Open the door, it's Amlan...

There's talk of new days.
In this season of hunger someone sows hope.
Only a gun can give you a mouthful to eat, they say.
A swarm of new flags swoops in
every mouth is stuffed with new slogans.
Someone lights a torch in the woods
The boots come trampling in the countryside
A sister cries mother o' mother
A brother's corpse is found
In wave after blood wave, Assam of the 90s flows

Dry air cracks with a boom.

I can't sleep

Someone walks by,
Someone taps on the bamboo wall.

I AM YET A MIYAH

Shajahan Ali Ahmed

Mine is the story of
A burning bone-crunching sun
My manhood the cautionary tale
Of bent shoulders
And the pricking of salted thorns
Mine is the story of
'Grow more food', man-eaters
Cholera, diarrhoea
And a fragrant revolution scattered by
My fathers
In a forest of thorns
Mine is a story of heroes.

Mine is the sacrificial offering of '61
Of blood screaming through
The binds of history
Mine is the story of '83, 90-94, 2008, 2012, 2014.

Mine is the oppression, the ignominy
The deprivation of Dravidians in Pragjyotishpur
I am the colour of a shame
Holding its ears, bending its knees

While kings and dynasties pass
I am the one under the fool's cap
Standing in line with dumb cattle

I am a painting of heritage
Hung in a stable
Because though the bottles look different
The wine is yet the same
And judging by birth alone, I am yet a Miyah.

DETENTION CAMP

Shajahan Ali Ahmed

With you in her womb the woman walked shyly among men.
A man gathered folds of virility and wore them around his
neck. You saw a new face and cried. They laughed. You learnt
to walk, talk and sing of spring and eternal monsoons. You
dreamt like a citizen of rice, clothes and a nest. There was talk
of you vanishing within the magical eyes of a princess, there
was talk of a downstream boat and your journey into the
kingdom of light.

Your sperm was to have a name
the bitter wind killed it all – in the light of the day, in full view.
A dark room waited for you but your address changed.
There was nothing different in your blood, nothing different
from them at least.

It is said that they love the sky – they keep alive tales of rain,
floods, drought and spring; of thirteen days, of twelve months.
Rakib chacha whose eyes go moist when you cry; his son sings.
'O my own land' and flowers rain upon him. You are not near
to hear him.

Your father, mother, brothers, sisters are all in this country and their prayers for you are stamped and mailed to a detention camp.

BROTHER, I AM A MAN FROM THE CHARS

Ashraful Islam

Brother, I am a man from the chars
On the Brahmaputra among *kohua*, *jhau-ikra*;
In the shade of *nal-khagori* is my jute-stick house.
People call me a *choruwa*, *bhatiya*, immigrant *shaykh*,
Neo-Asomiya, *Mymensinghia*,
Suspected Bangladeshi, non-aboriginal
Bangladeshi and what-not.

And though I was born in Assam and pride in
Calling myself an Assamese
The language doesn't slide down my tongue
My father wears a blue-checked *lungi*
My mother wears a *saree*
My sister wears *mekhela* or *churidar*
And me, brother, I wear jeans pants.

My father wears on his chin a handful of beard
A *topi* on his head, a string of beads on his hand, a jute bag on
his shoulders
But because he wears on his jaw broken Assamese,
He walks from work to the police station

Sometimes as a Bangladeshi, sometimes as a fundamentalist.
The big men say *chacha-chacha* and help him out of the lock-up.
The next day he's off to work again
To repay the hefty bribe.

OUR MOTHER HAS A D VOTE

Ashraful Islam

The sun is sinking
The red sky is turning black.
I have to go very very far
The road ahead is dark, very very dark.

Father has gone to the market
Mother has gone to the court.
She has a case hearing –
I am very very far from home.

There's nothing to eat at home.
The poor get government rice.
Our mother has a D vote,
So the rice for the poor is not for us.

Our sister has dengue,
Our brother is scrubbing glasses at a tea stall.
And I, standing on the public road
of a civilized society, cry.

No one sees, no one hears
No one sees, no one hears.

DON'T INSULT ME AS A MIYAH

Abdur Rahim

Don't insult me as Miyah anymore
I am ashamed to introduce myself
as Miyah no more.
You may love me
You may hate me
I lose nothing no more
I gain nothing no more
Don't insult me as a Miyah anymore.

You may love me
You may hate me
patronise me no more.
Pull me in your arms
and pin a dagger on my back no more.
Don't insult me as a Miyah anymore.

Look no more on my sunburnt back
for barbed wire scratches
but please, please don't forget '83, '94, '12, '14.
Please don't call my burns
the scratch marks of barbed wires anymore
Don't insult me as a Miyah anymore.

Please don't squeeze out my blood and ink ballads on
nationalism.
Don't peer into my mouth
the milk teeth are there no more.
Don't insult me as Miyah anymore

I am ashamed to introduce myself
as Miyah no more.

MY COUNTRY, YOU PROMISED

Abdur Rahim

My country, you promised
Blossoms of joy on our lips –
Now you don't even permit tears.

My country, you promised
Cheap food, clothes and homes –
You have made life cheap.

My country, you promised
The end of poverty –
Now the poor are ending.

My country, you promised
Employment papers in our hands –
You gave us a blind beggar's bowl and bell instead.

My country
If my sorrow is the primary basis of your joy,
I wish you all happiness –
Because I was born to bring happiness to others.

MY SON HAS LEARNT TO CUSS LIKE THE CITY

Siraj Khan

When I leave the chars for the city
They ask, 'Oi, where is your house?'
How do I say, 'In the heart of the Borogang'
Amid silvery sands
Flickering between stalks of jhau grass
Where there are no roads, no chariots
Where the feet of big men seldom fall
Where the air is a jhau green
There, there is my home.

When I leave the chars for the city
They holler, 'Oi, what's your language?'
Just as the tongues of beasts and birds
have no books, my language has no school
I draw a tune from my mother's mouth
And sing Bhatiyali.
I match rhythm with rhythm
Pain with pain
Clasp the sounds of the land close to my heart
And speak the whispers of the sand
The language of earth is the same everywhere.

They ask, 'Oi, what's your jati?'
How do I tell them that my jati is man
That we are Hindu or Musalman
Until the earth makes us one.

They try to scare me, 'Oi, when did you come here?'
I came from no 'somewhere'
When Bajan left the chars for the city
With a bundle of jute leaves on his head
With no reason, no rhyme the police jumped on him
And the examination
of pieces of paper began
Every time Bajan passed with laurels.

Just because he was a sandman
They gave him many, many colourful names:
Choruwa they called him, Pamua, Mymensinghia
Some called him a Na-Asomiya
And some 'Bideshi Miyah'
He carried these rashes on his heart
To his grave.

The rashes combined, raised their collective head and hissed
at me.

O mister snake charmer
How long will you slither and slide
My son goes to college now
He has learnt to cuss like the city
He knows little but he knows well
The sweet twists and the sweet turns of poetry.

EVERY DAY ON THE CALENDAR IS NELLIE

Abdul Kalam Azad

I live with a strange dream
I cannot sleep

Night glitters and my heart flutters
My ears pop like a rabbit's

On this new moon night I see
Every day on my calendar stained in blood
You have seen blood all your life, I tell my heart
Why are you scared of blood?

I close my eyes
Another handful of fear rumbles in my belly.

May is not marked in blood – the Beki's waters
Have washed it clean

I was scared in Khagrabari.
I walked through the Beki and reached Mazidbhita.

Haishyor's one and a half year old boy
Drowned
His body hardened
One fine day in June

Nearby uncle Fajal trembles like a leaf
Uncle has a fever, hasn't eaten for two days
He sits on a bamboo bed the size of a calendar
Aunty trembles like a leaf
What if the waters rise some more?

The wet calendar dries
Fear drenches my mind
In a dark room my hand turns the pages

A damned fox, maybe a civet, stole my hens
The cacophony of chickens strut over
My calendar

Sister Halimon has left her three month old child in Kokrajhar
Sister Hasina had her baby there
In four years the little boy has not known the outside of a coop

My world shivers in fear
I cannot sleep

Lend me some strength friends
Lend me some false hope

For one – just one – night on this calendar
Let me sleep.

FOR SEVENTY YEARS I HAVE BEEN AFRAID

Abdul Kalam Azad

For seventy years I have been afraid
This is not the fear of finding or losing you
I don't know.
No one else might know but Baba did
He knew the testament of my fear
Everyone else – uncles and the maulana uncle
Preached their own testament.

'Open your heart and love.'
'You are not one thread less or one thread more than anyone else.'
'You have the right to a heart full of love.'

They taught me that the corner of my heart
That held love for them should still remain,
That evicting them from that space would be
Unlawful, unethical and anti-conscience.
Seventy years have passed
Who listens to whom now?
A calamity has come over our land.
I have no father, no mother,

I walk around you in circles
Like an orphan.
I read a list of litanies
I talk about Baba, about my uncle,
But am scared to talk about maulana uncle
What if this is the trap to send me to Pakistan?
You don't hear, you don't see
You remain silent as a stone.
Then you say that you have turned into a robot.
All your love, all your fondness for me
You have packed in a box
A box sent adrift on the Brahmaputra.
I turn mad.
My anger, resentment and pride
Turn to ashes under my ribs.
It might be true that the pain in your heart
Is greater than mine
But you are grave as the sea
Your ripples don't show.
Some day you might stand on the Nilachal,
Might speak
'Come, come to my heart.'
Then I will look at you straight in the eye
I will find in your face my mother's face.

HEARTACHE

Johirul Islam

When I walk by the young ones say

'There goes the eternal patient'

'Wait, not eternal patient… the international patient! For many births, he has carried in his heart a deep deep pain.'

I say

'I am beyond medicine. The doctors have failed. I have forgotten how many sonograms I have done, how many x-rays I have taken.'

Karim's mother has a cure though, when she hears that the pain has risen to my chest.
She brings pictures of Nazrul and Rabindranath and holds them under my nose. The smell enters me and then I need no spells, no prayers breathed on my body.

Karim's mother says

'Get up now the pain has subsided'

I walk slowly towards the market.

THE FREEDOM OF SLAVERY

Rafiqul Islam

Whenever I feel like it
I drink a pint of freedom

Whenever I feel like it
I declare the classes dismissed,
Leave my master and become a master
Or maybe a fakir.
I will empty my copper bowl
Fill it with loose change
And open a roadside blessings stall.
I will sing ghazals and sell for cheap
The keys to heaven's gate.
Come for free grace and a mould
To expand your brain.

Whenever I feel like it
I will marry a bud lighter than a flower.
Whether they hit puberty or not,
I will make whores half-wives.
Who will say what, who will do what?
If I feel like it I will marry four times
Then say talaq thrice.

Whenever I feel like it
I will go to Guwahati, Shillong, Dimapur
I'll dig a pot of gold from a drain.

Whenever I feel like it
I will carry humanity on my back and cry out in the market.
At a rate of one per day I will sell
In Hatigaon, Katabari, Beltola Chariali
Pints of blood as cheap as water.
I will sell myself
For free I will sell the weight of my hammer
The sting of my sickle.

Whenever I feel like it
I change the city's geography
In the middle of a lake I make the moon
Stand on the moon's shoulders
And write on its back the many reasons why
I renounced my own for a forbidden love.

Whenever I feel like it
I burn at a bidi's other end,
Not in the bidi's fire.
I sit on my butt and in a chalk-drawing of a suicide
I fill my own body.

Whenever I feel like it
I am in the hut of the king of decadence
I lay a palm leaf mat – the moon sneaks
Through straw walls – and in the light
Of a Chinese lamp I roll dice and good whiskey.

Whenever I feel like it
I will lock my daughter's school
Announce a fiesta
Happy wedding – once, twice, many times.

Making up my mind is the way
Knowledge is fruitless.

We are the ones who plant
Thirteen-feet long seeds
In twelve-feet long melons
When we feel like it.

GRANDMA'S PET CROW

Rafiqul Islam

This monsoon a leaf returned to my mind –
A leaf I had crushed and let go in my grandma's time.

Grandma's pet crow is after my life
The crow caws and turns on me a tilted eye
It carries in its beak
The earth grandma scrubs off her hands
How can grandma bear it?

Rice and mustard have no peace –
When you step out of the storeroom
There's grandma's crow waiting for you,
A damned uninvited guest.

Even when there's no rice
The crow caws
Grandma's angry mouth becomes a microphone

'Die, you cawing crow, die'

Grandma says

'There's no rice for you, no mustard.
I pray for an unending flood.
I pray that all bamboo remains underwater.
Then I will see where you perch, you dead crow!'

So much water was never written on grandma's forehead
Not before she died, not after.
In grief my grandpa cut all the bamboo groves

When the waters swell something clicks in my head
Grandma's curse returns
Slowly the floor sinks, then the machan.
We carry our grief to the embankment
In grief the waters retreat.

The pet crow's perch never sinks.

KASHEM MIYA'S HEART

Rejaul Islam Bulbul

Kamalpur's Kashem Miya has a large knot on his lungi
His hands and feet are dirty
All over his body is the earth of Kamalpur.

Kashem Miya's blood, sweat and tears
Cut through the waters of Kamalpuria

His plough is in his fist all day,
The yoke on his shoulders.
If the knot on his lungi unwinds
If the yoke halts
Hunger will eat him first.

Kashem Miya's blood is sweet as honey
At night mosquitoes eat him raw
Before the sun rises the leeches of Kamalpur
Eat him
The dewanis frighten him with a D vote
The dewanis suck him dry

The OC at the thana says, send me your daughter, Kashem, or
she will see divorce.

The lawyer says, you have no NRC, Kashem, you will go to
Bangladesh.
Where should Kashem apply to let the world know that he has
no more blood?

Kashem adjusts in the morning, adjusts in the evening
The day grows small around him
The mud of Kamalpur says, how long will you cut me open,
Kashem?
I have blunted your plough.

Kashem says nothing, he cries.

He doesn't say it but I know
This late winter, no cat sleeps in his kitchen
The fire in his stove has remained unlit for days.

When a paper comes by post, Kashem comes running
What is this, he says, is it from the court?
Kashem's heart quivers like a leaf.
No, I say
But Kashem's heart is still a leaf.

FIRST, YOUR SHADOW

Abdul Mozid Sheikh

Let people say what they want
Let people do what they do
First, massage your shadow.

I know that you being around bothers no one
and no one being around bothers you.

If you don't plough
The fields remain barren
Rice vanishes from the market.
If you withdraw your hand
Vegetables vanish from the market
Buildings disappear in the cities.
If your foot is stalled
The wheels of rickshaws do not turn
The feet of the rich remain stalled.
If you don't go into the drains
The drains don't move
The bowels of babus remain blocked.

That doesn't make you pure like the Ganga
Because it's your nature to save every pie –

Your shirt remains torn
Your lungi remains your guard against winter
You can't wear the weight of good clothes.

It's in your nature to pull bags of sugar
and not know what sweetness is.
To sell milk for chillies
and curd for salt.
You burn your heart with bidis
and eat stale rice with a broken chilli.

It's in your nature
To push and pull your way around
To file case after case against your uncle
To feed cats and dogs on your hard-earned wealth.
Days will pass and you will be back
In labour camps
Calling this person a bastard and that person a rascal
and turning your own sons and daughters to skeletons.

It's in your nature
To puncture your children's noses
Before the smell of spices can reach them.
You don't have to look around, do you?

THE GAB TREE

Mohin Khan

The gab tree is dark all day
It swarms with ghosts at night
Everyone says it's the stork's tree
But look carefully
The gab is the kingdom of mongooses.

When a big eye fell on the gab tree's empire
Nana said he would cut the gab tree and make me a stool.

Nana died before his time
Thank God, the gab tree lived on.
I said, let me do nana's unfinished job
I somehow managed to evade the big eye.

But there was no gab tree,
No sign that it had ever stood
Our useless talk became sand
Where the gab stood
Was now a forest of reeds.

Nana made us, the old man!
All the hopes he had sown,

All the dreams he had promised –
That we would all sit on a gab stool

A lie.

The big eye had no business here
Our feet had no business shivering in hope.
We looked forward to the gab tree
All we got was a forest of reeds.

A TWO HUNDRED YEAR OLD SPRING

Ringkul Ahmed

1.
Somewhere is a valley where for two hundred years, there's no
rain and only a two hundred year old spring. There's dead
heads of grass
and torn fibres. Ashes from burnt houses and black smoke.

2.
In the valley of a two hundred year old spring, a green
rebellion
comes every year and covers the valley in a green shawl.
In every alley, every gully, in every field is the smell
of the oozing of ripe potatoes, rice, jute, tomatoes and
tomatoes

3.
Look, look at the blue flags at the end of the char – they are lungis
fluttering on the stick figures of our uncles, their chests are bare.
Their backs burn in the sun and in the rains their houses burn.
All these uncles, all our Miyah uncles, hold in their hands
a fistful of ash.

WHY DO OUR POEMS SCARE YOU?

Aman Ali

For centuries I have been fighting for a fistful of rice
Fighting for a little space to rest my head.
Our poems are not against you
Our poems are against hunger.

Our poems do not know sedition
Do not know the politics of holy men
In our eyes float detention camps
One of which houses my mother
I write poems in my mother's tears.

If we ask for a little rice your plates will not be empty
If we plant a little shrub your gardens won't go dry
If we write a little verse your poetry doesn't shrink in dignity.

Our poems do not know servitude
Our poems have not learnt rebellion
How many times have you looked for concertina marks on our
backs
And sat us on your knees by the roadside?
Did we ever protest?

The river took our lands, our homes many many times
Did you see us protest?
I rubbed the tears out of my eyes
And went to Guwahati for work
The police caught me, I don't know why
And took my handprints.

I came home and found the court notices
And yet I didn't protest
I raised my hands to God and cried.

One poem of mine raises a thousand questions.
Remember this – I can't bear the shame of being called a
Bangladeshi anymore.
How will you understand the pain –
The pain of being asked to prove one's citizenship in one's own
motherland?

You win the test even if you don't sit for it
Go, ask my grandfather bending over his stick
How many times he has stood the test.

You can't bear one little poem!
Someday come to the shore of our grief
See with your own eyes
How the river bears away our bodies.

Why do you fear when we write poems
In the language we weep in?
The water in your eyes and mine is the same
Your grief and mine bears the same address

Your country and mine are bound within the same barbed wires.

We have lit this flame with the fires of our pain.
Why does this flame scare you?
This flame will never burn your home –
Your target and mine is the king's palace.

MY MOTHER

I was dropped on your lap, my mother,
Just as my father, grandfather, great-grandfather
Yet you detest me, my mother, for who I am.
Yes, I was dropped on your lap as a cursed Miyah, my mother.

You can't trust me   because
I have somehow grown this beard.
Somehow slipped into a lungi
I am tired, tired of introducing myself to you.
I bear all your insults and still shout,
Mother! I am yours!
Sometimes I wonder what did I gain by falling into your lap?
I have no identity, no language, I have lost myself,
Lost everything that could define me
Yet I hold you close
I try to melt into you
I need nothing, my mother.
Just a spot at your feet.
Open your eyes once mother
Open your lips
Tell these sons of the earth
That we are all brothers.

And yet I tell you again
I am just another child
I am not a 'Miyah cunt'
Not a 'Bangladeshi'
Miyah I am,
A Miyah.
I can't string words through poetry
Can't sing my pain in verse
This prayer, this is all I have.

OUR MA

Rehna Sultana

We call our ma 'tumi' and our baba 'anne'.
When I was younger I remember my mother
Bowing before baba like the poor masses.
She sometimes started but never completed
A sentence when baba was around
Before the sentence was finished
Baba had already left.

Our ma wanted nothing from baba
Other than to talk to him
Baba never had the time
Every time he had the same answer –
Do you think I have nothing better to do?
Why should I talk rubbish with you?

We called our ma 'tumi' and our baba 'anne'.
Our baba roamed with big men –
Too much business and always work and more work.
People gave him too much respect,
Called him to too many meetings
Ma stayed alone at home
Ma alone, waited for baba.

She was so small before baba
That when we were younger we never thought
Of calling her 'anne'.
We called our ma 'tumi' and our baba 'anne'.

Baba was bigger than God
So we saluted his shadow.
Ma was like an ant or a lesser human
Just like the other children our age
Our baba was like a tiger
We gave him the same adoration that the tiger gets in the wild.
We shook with fear before our father
We ran and hid in our mother's skirts
A hen's brood.

Ma would hold us in a tight embrace.
When we were younger ma was always scared,
Her eyes always seemed to be welling over.
I thought mother had an eye-disease and asked her.
She lied
What can I tell you daughter?
The smoke from the stove makes my eyes water.
I don't know if ma had a personal life
There was always work at home
There were always grandparents to care for.

I never saw baba hug ma
I don't know if he ever held her close
I don't know if he ever kissed her lips
Maybe they never did or else
Why would ma's lips be so dry?

I heard that ma was the teachers' favourite in school
That she was a great student
That she had a beautiful handwriting
That she sang very well.
At night when she held me to her heart and hummed
I felt the fires in ma's heart.

When I ask ma now she says
She did have dreams once
Now there's only harsh reality.
Sometimes at night ma would hold us close and cry –
Maybe she missed baba too much,
Maybe she loved him too much
She never said so with words.
They never found the time, she never had baba.

Now that time has passed.
Now I don't see the waters in ma's eyes anymore
Our ma is steadier now, stable as a stone –
The only thing that remains unchanged is her fear.
Now ma's fear is not for herself.
She doesn't want that we grow up in fear,
She doesn't want her life to go to waste with ours.
She wants us to bear our own names,
So that the dreams she dreamt should be fulfilled in us.

GHOST NATION

Gazi Rahman

In a station in Bihar a nation sleeps with what looks like a
hungry skeletal child by her side.
She has walked through cities barefoot, on an empty stomach.
Now silenced by hunger and thirst, she sleeps.

The child persists but the nation doesn't wake.
In this world of bricks and stones, where are the humans?
Do their bodies have souls?
Their hands and feet and mouths move but they are not alive.
They breathe in and breathe out, and take part in the game of
living.
Their conscience died, gave up its soul many births ago.
Now ghosts live in these houses of brick and stone.

Maybe it's sleeping the sleep of the proud?
For what has this nation given that nation except hunger?

STAY WELL, MY COUNTRY

Gazi Rahman

You should have put us on trains
The opposite happened
The train sat on us

Stay well, my country
I leave you bread
Soak it in my blood and eat it

Stay well, my country

How long will you be quiet
How many deaths
Will you silently mourn?

My country
You have contracted silence
Weevils have eaten your conscience

I don't mourn my death
I don't remember when last I was alive

Look after my old mother

Stay well, my country

There was no cart for me
When I was alive
Now hearses crowd my yard

I don't mourn my death
I mourn humanity

Keep the dream of a new country alive

Stay well, my country

COME, REPUBLIC

Mirza Lutfar Rahman

Come, Republic, let's ride you to hell.
A sudden death waits, arms outstretched
Come, let's pass through death and write the century's finest
song.

Republic, your trucks are full of workers
Their thousand stories, buried every day in this city.
On the road to hell this city walks insomniac nights
Clutching to its heart so many stories.

The howls of darkness die every night under the city's navel.
Decades pass and everyone turns spectator
Everyone stands tip-toe and looks silently over Republic's
broken eaves.

Take us, Republic – on the dark turn of an unknown road
let's die.
Let our bruised bodies be quartered, divided and shared.
Alive, we washed it in sweat; in death we'll wash in blood
this city.
Come, let me ride you to hell.

Your wheels are broken, Republic, your trucks' engines are dead.
In these trucks my father, mother, brother and sister were lumped,
Lumped like bags of rice. Day and night they chanted chants of survival.

Come, Republic, carry us on your bone-hard back.
Alive, we couldn't reach home, our corpses will be at peace now.
Alive, we couldn't tame your arrogance; what justice after death?

Heaven is too far from this city
Our struggle is now mud – take us to the garbage dump outside the city.
Come, Republic, dump us in your truck and ride us to hell.

AFTER MY DEATH

Heena Al Haya

After my death I will live as a tree
My fallen leaves a poet will save
As pressed leaves in the folds of a book
On my branches a wayfaring bird
Will sing a void-dispelling love song.

And as a river I will hear all sorrows, cry to them
And save my tears in myself –

I will witness the coming togethers
I will witness the falling aparts.

I will be an abandoned house
Whose warden never returns,
With broken windows battered
By cold winds from the sea.

After my death I will live as a boatman
I will sail over the horizon
Or wear paper wings and fly to mountain peaks.

After my death I will live on

As a dead language
With no script
With no poets.

I will be a handful of grain
Grain which kills hunger forever
So that no one has to sell their kidneys anymore.

After my death I will be a land
Where humans are costlier than cattle
Where a word of protest doesn't earn a bullet.

After my death I will live on
In those who know how to fight for a heritage,
In those who have homes but no country.

I will live on as the struggle of a tribe without a lineage.

THE RIVER NYMPH

Ameena Ahmed

If you ask me, I'll tell you
how I breathe and how I live
in this river's enigma.
    What I owe to the mighty waterway.
Banks laced with sand and stones and lush soil,
nourishes my fragile soul.
    If you ask me, I'll tell you
how the river nurtures me.
The river is the nymph,
that weave the gaps between
dearth and abundance.
    If you ask me I'll tell you,
that it feels like a surreal synthesis
of folklore and faith!
The tunes of river,
trace the song
of my ancestry.
    If you ask me, I'll tell you,
how with each curve it tells
the history of a forbidden race,
dissolved in patriotic blood.
    If you ever ask me, I'll tell you

the story of a raw sun,
rising slowly and powerfully.
This unchallenged authority
of the river,
over my existence fortifies me.
I stand high and say,
I was born here and
I'll be buried here.
          If you ask me,
I'll certainly tell you
The story of a forbidden race.

INDEPENDENCE DAY

Begum Asma Khatun

Apparently tomorrow is Independence Day.
In my village I see independence every day.
Songs of independence play daily
in Phulbanu's mother's empty rice pot.

When Phulbanu's mother enters the kitchen
her children flock around and say,

'Mother we are hungry.'

Independence rolls down Phulbanu's mother's eyes.
She looks at her children's faces
and takes out her old begging bag.
Inside the bag are songs of independence.

Phulbanu's mother has a stomach ache...
the doctor says there are stones inside,
they say that she needs an operation.

When Phulbanu's mother returns empty-handed
from her begging rounds, she thinks

'Better stones in the stomach than an empty stomach.'

On the bodies of the stones are engraved
Songs of independence.

Phulbanu's father has been at the detention camp
for three years. He can't sleep even in the darkness.
When night grows, Nelson Mandela walks in
and lulls him to sleep and says,

'Through this path independence will come.'

Phulbanu's mother's eyes are full.
She rubs her eyes with her aanchal and says,

'Child, independence is not ours
Independence is of the rich man
Independence is of the MLA and the minister.
For us it's the walls of detention.'

'Is this country not ours, mother?'

'The country is ours but not the kings.
People say when the king is blind
Darkness descends upon the country
When a king is blinded by faith
The rumblings of a death-dance sound in the land.'

'Mother, the country is ours, our rights are ours
I will sing the songs of independence.

Come king, come minister
I will make the country better.'

A star dislodges from the sky and falls in Phulbanu's eye
From her mother's eyes independence keeps flowing.

THE HISTORY OF STONES

Begum Asma Khatun

Sarabjan, observe the drowned stones...
Breath has long left them and yet
The river bubbles.
They cling to the spectre of life,
clutch the sands on the riverbed
and strain against the tide of time.

Darkness catches the end of day,
there's a burning corpse in the heart of night
and a galaxy of stars float away.
Sarabjan, the sun is trapped
in a snail's shell.

A blue whale swallows the stones,
its bile turns them to dust
and out flows the dust
in a torrent of vomit.
Sarabjan, you know the cycle
of dust, of stone.

The stones have eyes and hearts.
Every time the river hurts

all bloodied eras float on their tears,
tears who, on the pages of time, turn into oceans.

When I swim in those oceans, Sarabjan,
I see charred bones.
I see the theatre of expert debate
held by the land-dwellers.
I see the clapping of hands
of the large audience.

Sarabjan,
do you know the story of Kalidas?
He sat on a branch and hacked at the roots.
They do the same
They start a forest fire and speak of progress.

Sarabjan, you know how
the onanistic stones have kept
the river alive;
how the civilisation of the river banks,
not written into history,
lives life zygotic in the womb of time.

RECLAIMING

Songs

Take a walk in my alleyway,
laden with cobweb and dust,
all the wall-signs,
and the meandering river
will escort you to my vintage courtyard.
Though dingy-looking,
it is all painted,
drenched in colours.
But this vibrancy comes to an abrupt halt,
when you press yourself to that bright wall,
to make a way for a group of men,
carrying a corpse on their shoulders.
A few steps into the road,
you spot my parched ribs,
yearning for the dead glory of yesteryears.
You see my swollen eyes,
still fired up with the fire
of funeral pyre
of my forefathers.
You break away from your touristy spirit,
confronting the reality you'd rather not.
This is my alleyway, on a happy day,

though dingy-looking, it is all painted,
decked up in stars,
drenched in the glory of yesteryears.

IN DOUBT AND WORRY MY TIME HAS PASSED

Songs

In doubts and worry my time has passed
Oh, my troubles!

I built my house with great care
Thought I would live here forever
From somewhere came a storm
Left the straw and took my thatch
Oh, my troubles!

I planted a plant with great care
Thought I would eat its sweet fruit (o my mad heart)
From somewhere can a storm
And broke my tree in half
Oh, my troubles!

I built a plough and yoke
Thought I would grow gold on my land (o my mad heart)
From somewhere came a farmhand
Broke my yoke and left my plough
Oh, my troubles!

YOU ARE THE SONGBIRD OF MY SOUL

Songs

I am the doer of a hundred sins,
it is all my fault.
You – the songbird of my soul.

The day I first saw you,
I thought what would happen to me
I have surrendered my heart and mind to you
You are the songbird of my soul.

The more I stay without you
The more my mind cries for one glance of you
My soul doesn't understand anything without you
It only cries itself to unease
You are the songbird of my soul.

YOU ARE THE SONGBIRD OF MY SOUL

MAD RIVER

Songs

You mad river   in a strange illusion you have trapped me
In our happy lives   you have drawn a ravine.

You have taken someone's land
You have taken someone's tin house
You have taken my newly budding love

You mad river   in a strange illusion you have trapped me

In our happy lives   you have drawn a ravine.

Some of us go to Mondira
Some go to Goruchar
Some go to Norikata reserve

You mad river in a strange illusion you have trapped me

In our happy lives   you have drawn a ravine.

THERE'S NO OTHER; HE'S ONE

Songs

He comes and he goes –
Have you seen him?
There's no other; he's one.

Twelve letters in la-illaha
Twelve letters in Muhammad
Chant this kalima of twenty four letters
written without a nuqta.
There's no other; he's one.

The story of God and nabi uniting –
Is this kalima with no nuqta.
Nabi is bound in God's love;
Seeing the nabi is seeing God.
There's no other; he's one.

Seeking God I found nabi;
Friend of God, the nabi's face
If you have knowledge you will know
That they are strung on the same thread
There's no other; he's one.

I know that at wahdaniyat
There's no God, no nabi
Says Hasan, you will see yourself there
If Murshid Chand is your friend.
There's no other; he's one.

It is a pleasure to have been brought into the world of *Again I Hear These Waters*, curated by Shalim M. Hussain. Towards the end of this project, I was brought on by Kristen Vida Alfaro for a creative editing process with Shalim, and it was important that I pay close attention to the conversations surrounding this anthology by people such as Deborah Smith and Nabina Das.

Shalim and I wanted the final title to be evocative and simple, while also suggesting the political nature of the text in a safe way. I suggested that we evoke communal sharing, often with an oral tradition, to reflect on how the poems were originally circulated. We spoke about how water features heavily in this project – more specifically how bodies of water move. This is something that resonated strongly with Shalim and he wanted the title to reflect the rhythm of this movement. 'Again' is a semantic choice that brings us back to ideas of circulation and community.

The poems openly thrived in the editorial process. In 'Mad River' by Begum Asma Khatun we wanted the poetic form to feel like a rushing river within the white page. We chose an active present tense for the phrase 'newly budding love' to entrance the reader towards the proximity of flora, life and fecundity. Shalim spoke to me about how 'mad' was an attempt to repurpose and give derogatory words a new meaning, as is often the way with Miyah poetry. As Shalim says in his introduction, 'the word "Miyah" itself is derogatory street slang with implications of barbarism and otherness.' The wildness of the river is a specific type of madness, a coursing in and out, a mad river that has impulse and the ability for anger and intention. I was caught by an image of a 'strange illusion', in the way that rivers can offer visions in folklore, a mirage of strangeness, and how chimeric the water can be.

We had wonderfully gentle conversations about love and softness. Shalim spoke to me of his own poems within the anthology, such as 'My Love's Letters' where the images of softness and water intertwine. He told me how silk is of time and place, and this love should be silk (Muga silk) so that silken softness is of and with them. This attention to sensory and local detail runs throughout the entire anthology, asking readers to take note of 'stalks of jhau grass', of bamboo underwater.

Kazi Neel's 'Journey' lent itself to rhythm and flow. After the first stanza we chose to use lower case letters to signify urgency and escalation. The refrain of 'cotton drops' in the poem was moved to a separate line and mirrors the inversions that Kazi Neel cleverly used to create a poem that floats. This question of rhythm became paramount with Shalim and I, as we edited in sing-song to poems like Neel's 'Comrade' with moments like 'Someone drew a hammer / and a sickle / on his chest' echoing a lullaby, clear and strong. This helped us to explore the way that Kazi Neel lets the reader move with the poem towards the lone empty cycle. Rhythm and flow make the story.

The poets in this work are unafraid to share what they see. A quack doctor and a grim reaper are one in the poem 'Republic's Broken Wall', 'grim-quack'. These moments of discovery reflect the shrewd clarity of this anthology. Elsewhere, in 'The Freedom of Slavery' by Rafiqul Islam, we made an active decision to keep the most uncomfortable lines from 'pints of blood as cheap as water' to 'I will marry a bud lighter than a flower' to convey the sheer moral skew of the narrator and that of the aggressor.

In 'Heartache' by Johirul Islam – I was reminded of a moment in the poem 'Finding Leo' within *Sergius Seeks Bacchus* by Norman Erikson Pasaribu, translated by Tiffany Tsao. It was the inevitable turn of the poem's narrator to another kind of life, a living and unliving. The voice in Johirul Islam's poem turns and will 'walk slowly towards the market'. Here, the beauty lies in choice, in turning to and walking towards something else – towards bustle, towards life. Indeed, choice is at the heart of this anthology. The ability to move towards a life, and to live true.

With warmth,

Tice Cin

ACKNOWLEDGMENTS

I thank all of the poets in this anthology for allowing me to translate their poems. Many of these poems went into multiple drafts, sometimes without the support of the original. I apologise for any over-translation. Thank you, Deborah Smith, for commissioning the book, and Tilted Axis and Kristen Vida Alfaro for publishing it.

The manuscript went through multiple editors and I thank all of them for their help, especially Tice Cin. Thank you, Tice, for reading the poems with me on Zoom, oohing and aahing at exactly the correct points and offering your extremely valuable input. I can't thank you enough for redrafting some of the translations and really opening them up.

I translated many of these poems as a Charles Wallace Creative Writing and Translation fellow at the University of Trinity St David, Wales in 2020. I thank Alexandra Büchler, Elin Haf Gruffydd Jones and Cari Lake for your love and hospitality. I miss you all. A piece of my heart is at the Lampeter railway station where we said our goodbyes, Elin.

Shalim M. Hussain

This book has been selected to receive financial assistance from English PEN's PEN Translates programme, supported by Arts Council England. English PEN exists to promote literature and our understanding of it, to uphold writers' freedoms around the world, to campaign against the persecution and imprisonment of writers for stating their views, and to promote the friendly co-operation of writers and the free exchange of ideas. www.englishpen.org

This edition published in the United Kingdom by Tilted Axis Press, 2024.

tiltedaxispress.com

ISBN (paperback): 9781911284925

ISBN (ebook): 9781911284918

A catalogue record for this book is available from the British Library.

Cover Art: Euphemia Franklin

Cover Design: Amandine Forest

Art Direction: Tice Cin

Typesetting and E-book production: Abbas Jaffary

Editors: Tice Cin, Nabina Das, Kristen Vida Alfaro (Editor's Note)

Proofreader: Mayada Ibrahim

Acquiring Editor: Deborah Smith

Publishing Assistant: Nguyễn Đỗ Phương Anh

Marketing Manager: Trà My Hickin

Managing Editor: Mayada Ibrahim

Rights Director: Julia Sanches

Publisher: Kristen Vida Alfaro

Made with Hederis

Printed and bound by Clays Ltd, Elcograf S.p.A.

ABOUT TILTED AXIS PRESS

Tilted Axis publishes mainly work by Asian and African writers, translated into a variety of Englishes. This is an artistic project, for the benefit of readers who would not otherwise have access to the work – including ourselves. We publish what we find personally compelling.

Founded in 2015, we are based in the UK, a state whose former and current imperialism severely impacts writers in the majority world. This position, and those of our individual members, informs our practice, which is also an ongoing exploration into alternatives – to the hierarchisation of certain languages and forms, including forms of translation; to the monoculture of globalisation; to cultural, narrative, and visual stereotypes; to the commercialisation and celebrification of literature and literary translation.

We value the work of translation and translators through fair, transparent pay, public acknowledgement, and respectful communication. We are dedicated to improving access to the industry, through translator mentorships, paid publishing internships, open calls and guest curation.

Our publishing is a work in progress – we are always open to feedback, including constructive criticism, and suggestions for collaborations. We are particularly keen to connect with Black and indigenous translators of Asian and African languages.

tiltedaxispress.com
@TiltedAxisPress